LEGALIZING
MARIJUANA

Essential Viewpoints

LEGALIZING
MARIJUANA

BY KAYLA MORGAN

Content Consultant
Ari VanderWalde, MD, MPH, MBioethics
Fellow in Oncology, Los Angeles, California

ABDO
Publishing Company

CREDITS

Published by ABDO Publishing Company, 8000 West 78th Street, Edina, Minnesota 55439. Copyright © 2011 by Abdo Consulting Group, Inc. International copyrights reserved in all countries. No part of this book may be reproduced in any form without written permission from the publisher. The Essential Library™ is a trademark and logo of ABDO Publishing Company.

Printed in the United States of America,
North Mankato, Minnesota
052010
092010

♺ THIS BOOK CONTAINS AT LEAST 10% RECYCLED MATERIALS.

Editor: Amy Van Zee
Copy Editor: Paula Lewis
Interior Design and Production: Christa Schneider
Cover Design: Christa Schneider

Library of Congress Cataloging-in-Publication Data
Morgan, Kayla.
  Legalizing marijuana / Kayla Morgan.
      p. cm. — (Essential viewpoints)
  Includes bibliographical references and index.
  ISBN 978-1-61613-523-2
  1. Marijuana—Law and legislation—United States. 2. Drug legalization—United States. I. Title.
  KF3891.M2M67 2011
  345.73'0277—dc22

                          2010002655

TABLE OF CONTENTS

A worker at a California medical marijuana dispensary displays various types of marijuana.

FEDERAL POLICY CHANGE

On October 19, 2009, U.S. Attorney
General Eric H. Holder Jr. issued a
memorandum that made news headlines nationwide.
Holder announced the federal government would
no longer make it a priority to prosecute marijuana

users who were breaking federal laws but complying with their state laws regarding marijuana.

Those who support the legalization of marijuana were thrilled by the U.S. attorney general's announcement. The director of the American Civil Liberties Union's Drug Law Reform Project, Graham Boyd, called the new policy "an enormous step in the right direction and, no doubt, a great relief to the thousands of Americans who benefit from the medical use of marijuana."[1]

Those opposed to legalizing marijuana were not pleased with Holder's announcement. Many were against the legalization of drugs, including marijuana. U.S. Representative Lamar Smith of Texas stated, "By directing federal law enforcement officers to ignore federal drug laws, the administration is tacitly condoning the use of marijuana in the United States."[2]

Different Administrations

When a new U.S. president takes office, major changes in legislation often occur. Laws are created that reflect the beliefs of the president and his or her political party. President George W. Bush (2001–2009) emphasized enforcing federal laws against marijuana. Federal agents raided medical marijuana dispensaries, doctor's offices, and marijuana gardens, some of which complied with state laws.

When Barack Obama became president in January 2009, a new administration was created. Under the Obama administration federal agents would no longer raid medical marijuana dispensaries complying with state laws. The federal government would also not prosecute marijuana users following state laws. However, cases that involve unlawful possession, use of a firearm, sales to minors, or money laundering would be investigated.

Conflicting Legislation

Holder's memorandum highlighted how differences between federal law and state law about marijuana can be confusing and cause conflict. Currently, marijuana is an illegal drug on the federal level. It is listed as a Schedule I substance under the U.S. Controlled Substances Act. According to the U.S. Drug Enforcement Administration, this means marijuana has "a high potential for abuse, no currently accepted medical use in treatment in the United States, and a lack of accepted safety for use . . . under medical supervision."[3]

But state laws also exist regarding marijuana, and not all of them align with the federal law. For example, California legalized marijuana for medical purposes in 1996. Physicians and medical research professionals reported that marijuana use might have some health benefits for people with certain medical problems, such as nausea or migraines. Some lawmakers, who had long considered marijuana use to be only harmful, changed their minds based on these reports. However, other medical reports maintained that marijuana's medical benefits are marginal at best. They said the health risks of using marijuana negate any potential benefits.

Many people are undecided about medical marijuana because of this conflicting information coming from health experts.

California was the first of several states to legalize medical marijuana. As of 2010, 15 states have made allowances for marijuana use for medical purposes. These states are Alaska, California, Colorado, Hawaii, Maine, Maryland, Michigan, Montana, Nevada, New Jersey, New Mexico, Oregon, Rhode Island, Vermont, and Washington.

THE HEART OF THE CONTROVERSY

In addition to medical considerations, the

Opposing Views on Health Risks

Many medical professionals express their opinions on the health risks of marijuana. They base their opinions on scientific research. Sometimes, their opinions—and even their research—differ. For example, in 2002, the British Lung Foundation published a report on the effects of marijuana on respiratory health. The report compared smoking 3 to 4 marijuana cigarettes per day with smoking 20 or more tobacco cigarettes per day. The foundation found that marijuana smoking is comparable to tobacco smoking with regard to bronchitis, or inflammation of the bronchial tubes, lung infections, and damage to bronchial mucus. Marijuana smoking also likely weakens the immune system of the smoker.

However, a large study presented by the American Thoracic Society in 2006 reported that even heavy users of marijuana had no increased risk for lung cancer. Additionally, marijuana advocates point out that heavy marijuana smoking is rare. Smoking even 3 or 4 marijuana cigarettes per day is very uncommon, whereas 20 tobacco cigarettes per day, which is one pack, is a common rate of smoking.

marijuana debate has other facets. The discussion also includes moral beliefs, legal perspectives, and economic considerations.

Although buying, selling, growing, using, or possessing marijuana is legal in some states, it is illegal in most cases. Statistics estimate that more than 65 million—about one in every five—Americans use the drug occasionally or regularly. Some people look at these statistics and conclude that the United States needs to crack down harder on all of these lawbreakers. Others think that if so many people believe marijuana use is acceptable, our laws should change to reflect that. The scope of the issue makes it impossible to ignore.

Legalizing marijuana is a moral issue for people on both sides of the debate. Many opponents believe using marijuana is morally wrong because it alters a user's mental state and can lead to dangerous actions and addictions. They believe by legalizing marijuana, the government would be condoning an immoral practice. Furthermore, they believe keeping marijuana illegal is a strong statement that society in general will not allow dangerous and rebellious activities to become the norm. They believe marijuana use can be associated with laziness

Although some want to legalize marijuana for medical purposes, many people in the United States smoke marijuana recreationally.

and lack of responsibility. Keeping marijuana illegal is a way to protect families and communities from harmful behaviors that would reduce productivity and responsibility.

On the other hand, many who favor legalization believe people have the moral right to make their own choices about what to do with their bodies. Supporters believe prohibiting marijuana use violates the First Amendment right to freedom of expression. Some believe that making forms of self-expression illegal, such as smoking marijuana, limits a society's growth, creativity, and advancement.

A Popular Drug

According to the National Organization for the Reform of Marijuana Laws (NORML), marijuana is the third most popular recreational drug in the United States (behind alcohol and tobacco). According to government surveys, at least 25 million Americans smoked marijuana in 2008 and more than 14 million use marijuana regularly, despite the laws against it.

From a legal standpoint, the key issue in the debate regards harm to U.S. society and determining which is worse: marijuana use or laws preventing it. While the U.S. Constitution protects individual freedoms through the Bill of Rights, laws also exist to protect the health and safety of all citizens. Some people believe that, in the case of marijuana, the goals of individual freedom and protecting the public are at odds. Others believe one goal is clearly more important than the other.

Economics have become another piece of the debate. In the first decade of the twenty-first century, with the U.S. economy struggling, lawmakers began to think hard about how the nation is using its diminished resources. Lawmakers began looking for ways to bring in more money and spend less. As a result, the debate over the legalization of marijuana has been reenergized. Proponents believe legalizing marijuana would create a great deal of income in the form of tax revenue, as the sale of the drug would be taxed as in any other legal business. They also believe changing the law would save on spending. In their view, marijuana is not very harmful, and the money spent to keep marijuana illegal by arresting, prosecuting, and imprisoning offenders could be better used elsewhere. Proponents of legalization believe police time and resources could be better spent tracking down much more dangerous criminals.

Opponents of legalization use an opposite economic argument. They believe the short-term gain from taxing marijuana would be negated by an expected increase in violent crimes as a result of more people using drugs. Society would have to put more resources into the police force and prison systems, and people would have to spend more money on personal security to protect themselves from a large population of drug addicts. Furthermore, these addicts would not be contributing productively to society, and the economy would be losing the contributions of otherwise able bodies and minds.

Use of Police Resources

According to the Marijuana Policy Project (MPP), a group that seeks to reform laws regarding marijuana use: "Someone is arrested for a marijuana offense every 36 seconds. . . . Eighty-nine percent of these are for marijuana possession—not for sale or manufacture. [And, in] the U.S., there are more arrests for marijuana possession each year than for all violent crimes combined."[4] However, some people wonder how many violent crimes are prevented by arresting people for marijuana use.

There are many unresolved issues in the marijuana debate. Discussion continues about marijuana as a safe medicine, the constitutionality of laws restricting personal drug use, and the morality of its use. Lawmakers continue to face the challenge of addressing these medical, legal, moral, and economic issues as they create new laws regarding marijuana.

For some people in the debate, the issue of who decides is a serious one. It highlights the rights of individuals, the role of lawmakers and the government, and who should dictate policy. It is a matter of determining what takes precedence: the law or individual choice. But the matter of law is complicated as well. There are federal laws and state laws, and they sometimes conflict. Lawmakers, organizations, physicians, and private citizens hold many varying opinions about marijuana legislation. Resolution continues to be a challenge. ⌐

Breaking the Law as Protest

Some people in favor of marijuana legalization feel so strongly that they break the law in support of their beliefs. A few people in favor of marijuana legalization have intentionally smoked marijuana in public to protest current marijuana laws. This is a serious problem for lawmakers. The issue brings up questions regarding how to deal with laws and individual beliefs when they do not align. For example, some question whether all citizens should follow the law regardless of their individual beliefs about marijuana. Others wonder if the law should change to accommodate public will.

Attorney General Eric H. Holder Jr.'s memorandum highlighted differences between federal and state laws regarding marijuana.

Cannabis leaves

THE CANNABIS PLANT

Marijuana is one of the most commonly used drugs available in the world today. Despite the fact that it is an illegal substance in many countries, marijuana use is nearly as widespread as that of tobacco, alcohol, and painkillers such as aspirin. The effects of smoking marijuana vary from person to person. These can range from feelings of happiness and well-being to feelings of anxiety and panic. Marijuana lowers a person's inhibitions and ability to concentrate and can impair judgment.

ORIGINS

Marijuana is harvested from the plant *Cannabis sativa*, which is informally known simply as cannabis or the hemp plant. Cannabis is believed to have originated in central Asia. There, it grows wild from Iran to Siberia. The substance has been discovered in tombs dating to 8000 BCE. And records in China detail farming hemp for its fiber as early as 2800 BCE.

Ancient peoples likely came upon the plant while foraging for seeds, nuts, and fruit. Early Asian empires made use of cannabis for its medicinal properties and mind-altering effect, and they took advantage of the fibers in its stalk.

Naming Marijuana

Botanist Carolus Linnaeus gave the cannabis plant its full scientific name, *Cannabis sativa*, in 1753. It had been known as cannabis for some time, but the addition of *sativa* (Latin for "cultivated") made the plant an officially classified species.

Marijuana has acquired many nicknames, including pot, weed, grass, dope, ganja, skunk, and wacky tobaccy. Nicknames for a marijuana cigarette are equally widespread and include joint, doobie, reefer, spliff, blunt, bomber, and roach. The word *marijuana* is sometimes spelled with an *h* instead of a *j*: marihuana.

The hemp plant is highly versatile, which may have helped its spread across the globe. Hemp grows throughout the world in temperate and tropical regions. It can adapt to different environments and has grown around the edges of the Sahara, Gobi, and Taklimakan deserts for many centuries. Hemp can also thrive at high altitudes. It even grows wild in North America.

Many Uses

The hemp plant is valued for myriad uses, many of which are industrial. Different parts of the plant are used to create a variety of products.

Plant-Based Drugs

Two groups of plants contain psychoactive compounds. One group produces psychotropic drugs, which affect the central nervous system. The other group produces psychotomimetic drugs. These drugs mimic psychosis by affecting the mind in a manner that alters perception, sometimes through hallucinations. Cannabis is part of the second group.

Oil from hemp seeds is edible and high in protein and essential fatty acids, making it a suitable dietary supplement. Hemp seeds and oil are not psychoactive and do not produce a high. Hemp seed oil is also used to create cosmetics and pharmaceuticals. The oil has technical applications and is used to create plastics and paints.

Hemp seeds have other uses as well. In addition to being used whole by growers who cultivate hemp, when

Hemp can be used to make clothing. Designer Raina Blyer created this hemp blend skirt.

hulled, hemp seeds can be consumed. Toasted, they are a snack when eaten alone, or they can be added to baked goods and granola. The seeds have been used during emergency food shortages in places such as China. They can also be processed into nondairy cheese and milk. Consumption of hemp seeds extends beyond humans. It is often included in bird and pet foods.

The stalk of the plant is also harvested for other uses. Plant stalks are soaked in water until they break down enough to be separated into strands known

Hashish

Hashish is another drug that can be harvested from the cannabis plant. It is made from just the plant resin and resin glands. The plant's flowers are rubbed until the resin comes off. Then, it is pressed into blocks for later use. Historically, cannabis resin was collected by hand. Today, a sieve allows the resin from the flowers to be mechanically filtered and processed. Hashish has a higher THC content than marijuana—up to 20 percent in its strongest form—which makes it a more potent substance.

as bast fibers, which are referred to simply as hemp. These fibers are used to make a variety of items, including rope, cloth, paper, insulation, and flooring.

Marijuana

Just as the stalk and the seeds of the hemp plant have uses, so, too, do its leaves and flowers. Marijuana comes from these parts of the plant, which contain a substance known as tetrahydrocannabinol (THC). THC gives marijuana its psychoactive properties. Other less-potent substances within cannabis also have mind-altering properties. THC and all of these substances are called cannabinoids.

After harvest, the leaves and flowers are dried, crushed, and stored for later use. Small amounts of marijuana may be stored loose in bags or other containers. Larger amounts are often compressed into bricks, and very large amounts may be tied in giant bales.

Cannabis leaves contain much less THC than do the flowers or buds, making marijuana that comes solely from the leaves less potent. Marijuana made with only the flowering tops of the cannabis plant is considered by users to be of the highest quality. It has a special name—*sinsemilla*. Often, a combination of the leaves and flowers or buds is used, which helps explain why marijuana from different sources may have very different potency.

In addition to being used for its mind-altering effects, some people use marijuana for medical reasons.

A Versatile Plant

Hemp, like many plants, has more than one variety. Botanist George Watt wrote about these differences in 1889:

"A few plants . . . seem to have the power of growing with equal luxuriance under almost any climatic condition, changing or modifying some important function as if to adapt themselves to the altered circumstance. . . . [H]emp is perhaps the most notable example of this . . . it produces a valuable fibre in Europe, while showing little or no tendency to produce the narcotic principle which in Asia constitutes its chief value."[1]

Hemp plants can reach as tall as 16 feet (5 m), and height varies by type. Hemp grown for its fiber tends to be shorter, ranging from 6 to 10 feet (2 to 3 m). Seeds of this variety are planted close together, and these plants have almost no branches. Hemp grown for its oil or drugs is planted differently. It grows differently as well. It is shorter and has a lot of branches. Plants in this variety are planted farther apart.

Hemp's global viability has resulted in many names. The Chinese call it *ma*, and the French call it *chanvre*. Hemp is known as *kannabis* in Greece and *canapa* in Italy. Hemp is called *hanf* in German and *canamo* in Spanish.

"Early man experimented with all plant materials that he could chew and could not have avoided discovering the proper- ties of cannabis, for in his quest for seeds and oil he certainly ate the sticky tops of the plant. Upon eating hemp, the euphoric, ecstatic and hallucinatory aspects may have introduced man to an other-worldly plane from which emerged religious beliefs, per- haps even the concept of deity. The plant became accepted as a special gift of the gods, a sacred medium for communion with the sacred world and as such it has remained in some cultures to the present."[2]

—*Richard E. Schultes, from* Man and Marijuana, *1967*

Some doctors believe marijuana is useful to people with cancer, glaucoma, anxiety, migraines, multiple sclerosis, and acquired immunodeficiency syndrome (AIDS). This scientific belief aligns with centuries of folk wisdom about marijuana's healing properties. The substance has a long history of medical application. It has been thought useful as the following treatments: analgesic, anesthetic, antidepressant, antibiotic, and sedative.

As with the other facets of the marijuana debate, the medical effectiveness of marijuana has opposing viewpoints. A large number of medical experts believe marijuana is addictive and harmful. What the United States will legislate regarding marijuana will be due in large part to what is decided about its medical merits. But as history has shown, U.S. laws about marijuana use have been based on more than a single issue.

These marijuana bricks were found in Florida during an undercover drug bust. The bricks were hidden in furniture.

Hemp seeds

HISTORY OF CANNABIS
USE AND LAWS

he hemp plant has been widely used for centuries. The debate over what to do about this plant and its by-products has been a long one and is ongoing. The argument has taken many forms throughout the years, and the focus has changed

depending on the social values of
the time.

CANNABIS AND ANCIENT RELIGION

Early Asian religions used the
hemp plant in a variety of ways, and
the Buddhists revered it. Throughout
western Europe, the hemp plant was
famed for its healing properties,
which many considered magical. In
some places, hemp was burned as a
way to ward off illness and disease.
Farmers fed hemp seeds to livestock
to encourage good health, but the
plant was not used specifically as an
intoxicant or drug.

The widespread belief in the
hemp plant as a magical herb
eventually led some people to believe
it was a tool of witchcraft. This led
the Christian church to label hemp
an evil plant. Beginning in about the
eleventh century, several centuries
of witch hunts began in Europe, and

"Shamanistic traditions of great antiquity in Asia and the Near East had as one of their most important elements the attempt to find God without a vale of tears; that Cannabis played a role in this, at least in some areas, is borne out in the philology surrounding the ritualistic use of the plant. Whereas Western religious traditions generally stress sin, repentance, and mortification of the flesh, certain older non-Western religious cults seem to have employed Cannabis as a euphoriant, which allowed the participant a joyous path to the Ultimate; hence such appellations as 'heavenly guide.'"[1]

—William A. Embolden Jr., "Ritual Use of Cannabis Sativa L"

anyone growing or using the plant was suspect. The Roman Catholic Church outlawed hemp during the Middle Ages. This ban was eventually lifted in several areas, but the antihemp belief remained among many Christian groups and others in society.

HEMP USE SPREADS

The witch hunt hysteria eventually faded, and the usefulness of the hemp plant could not be denied. By the sixteenth century, British monarchs were requiring all landowners to grow hemp for industrial purposes. As trade avenues expanded throughout Europe, Africa, and Asia, the use and trade of hemp and its products spread. Shipping channels became more active, and overland routes strengthened as transportation technology developed.

Throughout the British colonies during the seventeenth and eighteenth centuries, law required the cultivation of hemp. American colonists grew hemp and shipped

Hemp in Sixteenth-century Europe

By the sixteenth century, European nations had discovered the importance and usefulness of hemp. In 1563, England's Queen Elizabeth I ordered all landowners with at least 60 acres (24 ha) to grow hemp. If they did not, they had to pay a fine. In 1564, King Philip of Spain ordered hemp to be grown throughout the Spanish Empire.

it across the Atlantic Ocean for processing. Hemp became one of the most valuable products in the colonies. By the eighteenth century, the British East India Trading Company had begun taxing hemp sales in India, another British colony.

In the American colonies, frustration grew in response to Britain's taxes on hemp. The colonists there believed the laws and taxation policies Britain imposed upon them were unfair and extreme, which prompted the American Revolution. The colonists wanted independence—freedom from British rule. Hemp became one of the disputed products, along with tea, cotton, and flax. The colonists were angry that they were forced to grow hemp but not allowed to use it to make products. Instead, they were required to send the raw crop back to England, where it would be processed and turned into clothing, paper, rope, and other essential products.

Founding Fathers' Views

During the years prior to the American Revolution, the industrial uses of hemp were considered very important, and it was a popular commodity in the American colonies. The men responsible for the Declaration of Independence and the U.S. Constitution generally promoted the practicality and usefulness of the hemp plant. Thomas Jefferson believed hemp was a vital crop. He had brought hemp seeds to the colonies from France. George Washington agreed. He once told the caretaker for his land and homestead at Mount Vernon, "Make the most of the hemp seed. Sow it everywhere."[2]

The British then shipped the finished goods back to North America. After the American Revolution, the American patriots were able to manufacture cloth, paper, and other items from hemp grown in the colonies. This helped them become less reliant on imported goods from Europe.

Marijuana as Medicine

In the late eighteenth century, marijuana began appearing in medical reference texts. It was recommended for treating coughs and general pain and as an analgesic to soothe allergies. These uses had their roots in ancient folk remedies and beliefs about the substance.

By the middle of the nineteenth century, various forms of marijuana were available for general purchase in the United States. This was before medications needed to pass a strict set of criteria demonstrating they were both safe and useful before physicians could prescribe them. Most medicines were available to anyone who walked into a chemist's shop and asked for them. Doctors recommended certain treatments for patients, but drug purchases were far less regulated than they are today.

During the late nineteenth century, people used machines to make sisal hemp rope for industrial uses.

A pill form of marijuana that contained hashish was developed and used as a painkiller and antibiotic. As pharmaceutical companies grew larger and medical science advanced, synthetic painkillers such as aspirin were developed in laboratories. Doctors and scientists became uncomfortable with prescribing substances with unknown potencies and unpredictable side effects, and thus began to turn to the laboratory to produce more predictable medicines.

A Shift in Use and Attitude

In the decades immediately following the Civil War, people started using marijuana for recreational purposes. For a time, this was considered socially acceptable. In some circles, marijuana use was even considered safer than alcohol use, because marijuana tended not to trigger recklessness or violence.

In the early twentieth century, U.S. social attitudes toward drugs began to shift. In 1906, the Pure Food and Drug Act labeled marijuana as a dangerous drug, alongside opium, morphine, and cocaine. This law required all medicines containing these drugs to be clearly labeled. The law did not make marijuana illegal, but it was certainly a strong step toward labeling marijuana a dangerous substance.

Marijuana began to be seen as a drug of the lower classes. Poor Mexican and Latin-American immigrants, African Americans, working-class members of all races, and creative types such as artists, writers, and musicians gained the reputation of being marijuana users. Some of this stereotyping came from racist or elitist attitudes. For upper classes, the once-accepted drug became undesirable, at least in public.

A group of citizens concerned about the influence drugs might have on society became determined to see all mind-altering substances made illegal, or at least unavailable. They were worried about the effect mind-altering substances had on the work ethics and values of drug users, and they were also concerned these drugs might cause irresponsible and possibly dangerous behavior.

In 1919, these moral activists earned a big victory. The Eighteenth Amendment to the U.S. Constitution

Why Prohibition Failed

In colonial America, alcohol was inexpensive and often cleaner to drink than water or unpasteurized milk. In the early nineteenth century, the U.S. temperance movement began to urge men and women to limit their alcohol intake. But by the turn of the twentieth century, the temperance movement had grown quite strong in the United States. Many groups organized to promote the benefits of limiting the use of alcoholic beverages, which many believed to be addictive. Some people saw its use as immoral and sought to ban the substance entirely. The movement gained so much momentum that in 1920, legal Prohibition went into effect.

However, less than 15 years later, Prohibition was repealed. There are many reasons why Prohibition was not successful in the United States. Under Prohibition, alcohol was still available for illegal purchase, and the demand for it was high. Many people used alcohol for social and religious events. Before the law went into effect, many people had stocked up on alcohol. Others made their own alcohol in bathtubs. This alcohol was commonly called moonshine. Illegal clubs called speakeasies provided alcohol to patrons. Bootleggers were people who traded in illegal alcohol, and it was often smuggled in from other countries.

began Prohibition, a period in U.S. history in which alcohol was banned. The legislation made wine, beer, and liquor illegal to make, sell, buy, and drink. However, Prohibition was repealed by the Twenty-first Amendment, which passed Congress on February 20, 1933, and was ratified on December 5, 1933.

The issues Prohibition raised in the 1920s are very relevant to the marijuana debate today. They include questions of morality, right and wrong, the beliefs of a society versus those of an individual, and how laws should be decided—for the many or to accommodate the minority.

After alcohol became legal again in the United States in the 1930s, the attention of the U.S. public and law enforcement officials soon turned to another substance: marijuana. Harry J. Anslinger would make it his personal mission to see the drug eradicated from the United States.

Prohibition agents destroyed illegal barrels of beer in the 1920s.

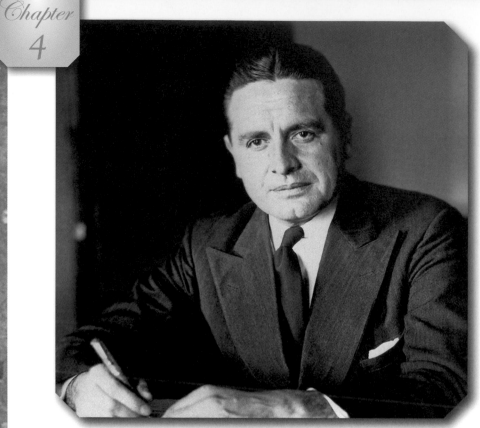

As commissioner of the FBN, Harry J. Anslinger campaigned to rid the United States of marijuana.

THE DEBATE BEGINS

In 1930, the Federal Bureau of Narcotics (FBN) was created under the U.S. Department of the Treasury. The new agency's task was to regulate and enforce laws governing legal and illicit habit-forming drugs in the United

States. President Herbert Hoover approved the appointment of Harry J. Anslinger as the first commissioner of the FBN.

Anslinger took his job seriously, and he had a particular dislike for marijuana. He wanted to rid the nation of the drug. He worked to increase public awareness of its health dangers and the harm it could cause to society.

Anslinger's campaign paid off. Seven years after he started his work at the FBN, a new piece of marijuana legislation was brought before Congress. The bill was named the Marihuana Tax Act of 1937.

The Marihuana Tax Act of 1937

In 1937, 46 states and the District of Columbia had laws against marijuana, but Anslinger and others wanted a federal law to take their place. The first federal legislation to attempt to control marijuana, the Marihuana Tax Act, was signed into law by President Franklin D. Roosevelt on August 2, 1937, and went into

Medical Marijuana under the Tax Act

Under the Marihuana Tax Act of 1937, physicians were legally allowed to prescribe marijuana to their patients. However, the prescribing physicians had to pay an annual tax to have a license to sell marijuana. They were also required to provide the government with details on each patient's identity and the nature of his or her illness. The notion of privacy between physician and patient was not considered important under the act. Many physicians and patients found this objectionable, and the medical use of marijuana decreased.

Doctor Woodward

Some people publicly opposed the Marihuana Tax Act of 1937, including Doctor William C. Woodward of the American Medical Association (AMA). He objected to the volume of doctors who had been arrested for treating patients with cannabis and claimed that some of the charges had been exaggerated. The AMA registered formal objections as the Senate debated the bill, but the Senate overruled the doctors' concerns.

effect on October 1. Those involved with marijuana importation, sale, production, or prescription were required to pay annual special taxes. When marijuana was transferred to another registered person who had paid the special tax, the fee was $1 per ounce. But when marijuana was transferred to an unregistered person who had not paid the special tax, the tax was set at $100 per ounce. At a time when a new car could be purchased for approximately $200, this was a huge amount of money. There were large fines imposed upon those who transferred marijuana without paying the associated fees. Those who were prosecuted for violation were tax offenders, not narcotics offenders. As a result of the Marihuana Tax Act, marijuana use became very expensive. The Marihuana Tax Act not only prevented people from accessing marijuana; it prevented growers from producing hemp for clothing and other uses.

WORLD WAR II

Though the federal government has not changed its position on marijuana use since 1937, it has shown a willingness to loosen the restriction on the hemp plant itself, at least temporarily. After the bombing of Pearl Harbor in 1941, when the United States entered World War II, the need for domestically produced fabric rose. The Philippine Islands, one of the United States' main sources of fabric, were now occupied by the Japanese. Despite the Marihuana Tax Act of 1937, the uses of the hemp plant were well known. Overlooking the fact that growing cannabis for nonmedical purposes was technically illegal, the U.S. government created the War Hemp Industries Corporation, which paid 20,000 midwestern farmers to grow cannabis for the government. More than 30,000 acres (12,140 ha) of cannabis were sown annually during the war years. Hemp was used for more than making fabric. Hemp seed oil became a lubricant for airplane engines.

The Attack on Pearl Harbor

The United States entered World War II when the Japanese attacked a major U.S. Navy base at Pearl Harbor, Hawaii. The war greatly impacted trade throughout the world, as nations that had once been trade partners became occupied by German and Japanese forces. U.S. efforts on the home front included a great deal of domestic production that generated new materials and resources.

The Grow Hemp for Victory campaign encouraged Americans to grow hemp to help the war effort. Today, legalization supporters look to this campaign to support their cause. If cannabis were so dangerous, they say, people would or should not have been encouraged to come in contact with it. Opponents of legalization disagree about the campaign's significance. Industrial hemp and marijuana cannot be equated, they say. However, because the two come from the same plant, opponents worry that making hemp legal will lead hemp growers to make and sell marijuana.

LEGALIZATION MOVEMENT

After the war, growing hemp was immediately banned. Yet, the illegal drug trade continued. By the 1960s and 1970s, a strong subculture surrounding marijuana use had developed. Even though the drug remained illegal on the federal level, people managed to get their hands on it. People from all walks of life—especially hippies, students, musicians, and soldiers—were interested in and used marijuana. Stores called head shops openly sold marijuana-related items, such as cigarette paper, pipes for smoking (called bongs), and cases for drug storage.

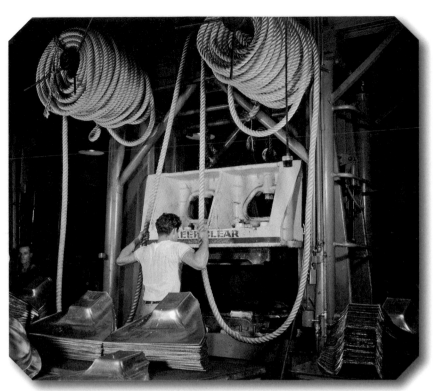

Hemp rope was used in factories during World War II.

Many people did not care that they were breaking
the law, but some wanted to see the laws changed.
Marijuana users began to organize. They did not
want to be seen as radical rule breakers but rather
as citizens with valid arguments for why marijuana
use should be acceptable. In 1971, a lobbying group
called the National Organization for the Reform
of Marijuana Laws (NORML) was established in

Washington DC. The legalization debate began taking on a new form.

Hippies

The hippie movement in the United States began in the 1960s on college campuses and continued into the 1970s. It spread to other countries, including Canada and England. Hippies were part of a counterculture that refused to adhere to traditional beliefs, which they believed were materialistic and repressive. Rather than focusing on rules and money, hippies promoted love, freedom, peace, and harmony, which they often symbolized by wearing flowers in their hair. Because of this, hippies are often called "flower children." Many hippies lived together in groups or communities and traveled throughout the country together, refusing to put down roots in any one place.

Hippies were easily identified by their appearance, which was characterized by long hair—including beards for men—brightly colored clothing, sandals, and beads. Women often wore flowing dresses.

The hippie movement was often associated with the use of marijuana, mushrooms, and other drugs. Many hippies used lysergic acid diethylamide (LSD), a powerful psychedelic drug that can cause hallucinations. Some speculate that drugs such as marijuana and LSD heavily influenced the ideologies behind the hippie movement.

The War on Drugs

During this time, the government continued to fight against marijuana and other illegal drugs. It created agencies designed to arrest marijuana growers, sellers, and users. Under President Richard Nixon, who came into office in 1969, combating illegal drugs became a high priority.

When Nixon announced his war on drugs, the government

strengthened its antidrug efforts. The Nixon administration established the Special Action Office for Drug Abuse Prevention and the Office for Drug Abuse Law Enforcement. Together, these agencies became the Drug Enforcement Administration (DEA), which remains active today. Between 1968 and 1973, the FBN was combined with several other government drug prevention agencies.

In addition, new legislation was created to fight drug use. In 1970, under the Controlled Substances Act, marijuana was labeled a dangerous drug. Following this act, numerous groups, including NORML, rallied against this label, claiming marijuana was a safe substance. In response to this increased federal control, some state legislation moved in the other direction. By 1978, at least 11 states had decreased their penalties for marijuana possession.

In the 1980s, President Ronald Reagan continued Nixon's war on drugs. However, at the time, more potent and addictive substances, such as cocaine, had come to the forefront of the fight. And in 1985, the U.S. Food and Drug Administration (FDA) approved Marinol, a synthetic drug containing THC, for treating side effects in cancer patients.

Now, there was a legal THC-containing drug that would supposedly give the same medicinal benefits as smoking marijuana. The creation of this new drug further fueled the debate over medical marijuana.

Marijuana use is often associated with the hippie culture
of the 1960s and 1970s.

In 2009, New Jersey Senator Gerald Cardinale spoke against a bill that would allow patients legal access to medical marijuana in the state.

MEDICAL MARIJUANA

*L*egalizing marijuana for medical purposes has received greater attention in the marijuana debate in recent years. Doctors have been observing people who take marijuana for decades and have at times noted that they experience relief from serious or chronic illnesses. Supporters contend that marijuana poses fewer risks than most legal medication and is difficult or even impossible to overdose on. In the states that make some provisions for legal medical marijuana, lawmakers have concluded that its benefits outweigh its risks.

MARIJUANA AND THE BODY

Smoking, eating, or drinking marijuana can create feelings of extreme happiness and well-being, calmness, and a different sense of time passing. The imagination becomes more active as the senses become heightened. The drug increases heart rate and blood pressure. The skin may grow warm, and the eyes may redden. Marijuana users often experience dryness of the eyes and the mouth, and their appetite is stimulated. It becomes harder for the user's mind to focus, and occasionally, feelings of paranoia can be overwhelming.

Some users experience one or more of these effects very strongly, while barely noticing others. Some people do not feel the effects much at all. These differences may depend on the user's physical chemistry, mood, expectations, or history of marijuana use.

HEALTH BENEFITS

Some doctors have determined that cannabis use may have positive effects for patients with certain ailments. In the introduction to *Cannabis in Medical Practice*, Mary Lynn Mathre, a registered nurse, states, "The cannabis plant (marijuana) . . . [has] therapeutic benefits and could ease the suffering of millions of persons with various illnesses such as AIDS, cancer, glaucoma, multiple sclerosis, spinal cord injuries, seizure disorders, chronic pain, and other maladies."[1] In the case of glaucoma,

The Question of Side Effects

Hospitals often give opiate painkillers, such as morphine, to patients. These drugs can be addictive and dangerous if used improperly. Even over-the-counter drugs can be problematic. Painkillers such as aspirin, which can cause stomach bleeding in some patients, and Tylenol may cause illnesses and have side effects.

When supporters of legalizing marijuana compare it to other drugs, especially painkillers, they point out the relatively few side effects of marijuana. NORML referred to a Canadian study in which investigators looked at clinical investigations and observational studies regarding marijuana use. The study concluded that marijuana users are at higher risk for "nonserious" adverse effects, such as dizziness, but did not find marijuana users to have a higher incidence of serious adverse effects.

Others disagree. They state that smoking marijuana subjects the user to potentially harmful side effects, such as an increased risk of bronchitis and emphysema. However, marijuana as a painkiller is still debated. Doctors are studying its possibilities as a painkiller and in what dosages.

a disease that causes fluid to build up in the eyes and can cause permanent vision damage, marijuana is thought to reduce the fluid pressure for patients. Marijuana is also thought to help prevent or reduce seizures in people with epilepsy.

People with AIDS suffer from a weakened immune system, which decreases their capacity to fight off disease and infection. This loss of the immune system can cause a decrease in appetite, weight loss, and malnutrition—symptoms that some believe may be relieved by marijuana. For cancer patients, marijuana has reportedly helped to minimize the pain and nausea associated with chemotherapy treatments.

However, some opponents believe marijuana does not have any legitimate medical or therapeutic benefits. They are concerned that people are basing their opinions about medical marijuana on personal

DEA Disagreement

In 1988, DEA Judge Francis L. Young wrote a 90-page decision about medical marijuana in which he stated, "Marijuana, in its natural form, is one of the safest therapeutically active substances known to man." He continued: "Nearly all medicines have toxic, potentially lethal effects. But marijuana is not such a substance. There is no record in the extensive medical literature describing a proven, documented cannabis-induced fatality."[2]

In 1992, DEA authorities overturned Judge Young's findings, citing political reasons for their decision. The agency did not specify what the political reasons were, but the result was continued approval for synthetic THC and a continued ban on marijuana.

accounts instead of medical science—and that these stories are creating harmful myths about medical marijuana. Dr. Mark L. Kraus of the Connecticut Chapter of the American Society of Addiction Medicine said:

> For those who are inclined to support medical use of marijuana, it is usually not the scientific evidence they consider, but only the unfounded self-reports of how marijuana relieved pain, chemotherapy-induced nausea and vomiting or HIV-AIDS Wasting Syndrome. . . . Proponents of the legalization of medical marijuana create the impression that it is a reasonable alternative to conventional drugs. But unlike conventional drugs, smokable marijuana has not passed the rigorous scrutiny of scientific investigation and has not been found safe and effective in treating pain, nausea and vomiting or wasting syndrome.[3]

HEALTH DRAWBACKS

The most important long-term physical effect of marijuana use is damage to the lungs from smoking. Asthma, bronchitis, and emphysema are lung ailments that may be caused or worsened by any kind of smoking. Those opposed to legalization emphasize these serious health risks. Those who

A man lights a marijuana cigarette at a California cooperative, a place where patients can safely access legal medical marijuana.

support legalization say marijuana does not have to be smoked to be effective. Marijuana can be baked into food and ingested or breathed in as a vapor. It can also be brewed with hot water to make tea. Therefore, the risk from smoking is simply a choice made by the user, much like the choices tobacco smokers make.

The body's response to the THC in marijuana can also put some people at risk for health complications. It can increase a person's heart rate and blood pressure, which could be problematic for someone with existing heart or circulation problems.

Appetite stimulation may not be a problem for healthy individuals, but a habit of overeating can lead to obesity, which could lead to many health problems.

Cannabis Addiction

There is considerable discussion about the addictiveness of marijuana. Dopamine, a chemical in the brain that causes feelings of happiness, is often blocked by drug use. The drug then takes the place of dopamine in the brain. Over time, the drug stops dopamine from being produced naturally. This causes addiction—the only way a user can feel good is by taking the drug. Some people argue that marijuana causes this kind of chemical addiction.

Studies show cannabis is not chemically addictive in the way heroin, nicotine, or caffeine is. This means the user's body will not go into a physical withdrawal if regular cannabis use is stopped. When a user stops taking a chemically addictive substance, withdrawal symptoms can include headaches, difficulty sleeping, nausea, or sweating.

However, even though marijuana users do not become chemically addicted, they may become psychologically addicted, which is also known as substance dependence. Although their bodies do not crave it, as is the case for users of heroin or nicotine, people may feel a strong mental desire to use it. Some cannabis users feel as though they need the drug to cope with difficulties in their lives and that the drug brings emotional relief. Some reports indicate that as much as 10 percent of habitual cannabis users may develop an emotional dependency on the drug. While the addictiveness of marijuana continues to be debated, most agree the drug has the potential to be misused. This worries doctors and lawmakers.

MARINOL

Many opponents of marijuana legalization do not believe the ban on the drug means doctors have to deprive patients of healing medicine. In 1985, the Unimed Pharmaceutical Company created dronabinol, a

Substance Dependence

According to the *Diagnostic and Statistical Manual of Mental Disorders* used by physicians and mental health experts, a substance-dependent person will show three or more of the following symptoms within a 12-month period:

• Increased tolerance for the substance
• Withdrawal symptoms—for example, restlessness, irritability, nausea, fatigue—when the substance is not available
• Increased usage
• Unsuccessful efforts to lessen or control use
• Spending considerable time trying to obtain, use, or recover from using the substance
• Giving up important social, work, or personal activities because of substance use
• Ignoring physical or psychological problems caused or worsened by the substance

Symptoms of Marijuana Withdrawal

Antidrug activists advise parents to keep an eye out for signs of drug use in their children. They suggest that some of the most frequently reported symptoms of marijuana withdrawal include restlessness, irritability, mild agitation, sleep disturbances, nausea, muscle cramping, and fatigue.

drug that contains synthetic THC. The drug comes in pill form and is marketed under the brand name Marinol.

For opponents of legalization, the THC pill is appealing for many reasons. It eliminates the drawbacks of smoking. Additionally, because the drug is created in a laboratory, it avoids the risks to public health brought about by bad crops of marijuana or diseases brought over the border along with smuggled drugs. Also, because Marinol is much less likely to create a high than marijuana, it is not alluring to recreational users. This lowers the chances of theft and other prescription drug abuses, such as using medication that was prescribed for someone else. Furthermore, opponents argue, marijuana, as it is currently used, has not gone through the scientific testing required for prescription drugs. Marinol is all that is necessary to grant patients the benefits of marijuana, if any benefits exist. In many people's opinion, Marinol makes the entire medical marijuana debate moot.

While those who oppose medical marijuana use find Marinol a viable solution, medical marijuana advocates believe there are many drawbacks to the synthetic drug. Those opposed to Marinol object to the fact that it deprives the patient of the euphoria delivered by marijuana, which they consider a powerful relief for chronic pain. And Marinol has been approved by the FDA only as an antinausea medicine or an appetite stimulant, not as a pain reliever.

Those opposed to Marinol also argue that it can be much more expensive than regular marijuana. Marinol capsules can cost as much as $200 per month. Some believe Marinol is more difficult to use effectively. Marijuana that is smoked gets to the bloodstream quickly, but oral doses take much longer to reach the bloodstream. Those in favor of the synthetic drug believe the potential cons of Marinol are worthwhile as a means to protect society from the dangers of legal marijuana.

Skeptics are also not quick to accept the idea of a synthetic substitute for a naturally occurring

Marijuana Anonymous

Much like the programs for recovering alcoholics, smokers, and gamblers, Marijuana Anonymous is a 12-step program that provides a support system for people recovering from marijuana addiction and abuse.

drug. According to NORML, a laboratory-developed version of THC may not be as effective as the original plant. Because cannabis contains many other chemicals in addition to THC, some people suggest that at least a portion of marijuana's healing properties may come from these other natural components.

Researchers John M. McPartland and Ethan B. Russo wrote in 2002: "Good evidence shows that secondary compounds in cannabis may enhance beneficial effects of THC."[4] They went on to explain that non-THC substances in herbal cannabis—cannabinoid and noncannabinoid—may be beneficial to patients by reducing THC-induced anxiety, deficits in the brain, and suppression of the immune system. Other elements of cannabis may help the brain by increasing blood flow and activity, killing pathogens in the lungs, and helping reduce inflammation.

Research on the biological effects of cannabis continues. Many of the chemicals in cannabis are not known, and it is unknown what role they play in marijuana's effect on the body. These chemicals might be helpful or harmful. ⌒

A woman protests to support the legalization of medical marijuana.

Some people want marijuana to be legalized and regulated as alcohol is, including age limitations and punishments for irresponsible use.

ECONOMICS, TAXATION, AND REGULATION

*D*iscussion of marijuana's medicinal merit has been ongoing for a few decades. Financial events have increased discussion of another facet of the legalization debate. With the onset of the worldwide economic crisis in 2007, Americans

from all walks of life became aware—
sometimes painfully so—of the
importance of saving money. For
some, this topic made the discussion
of marijuana legalization critical.

Lucrative Business

Supporters of federal marijuana
legalization are excited about the
possible economic benefit to the
United States. Taxation of marijuana
sales could produce millions of
dollars in annual revenue. The
additional money going toward state
and federal governments might
enable them to decrease their debts,
improve education, and enhance
current or provide additional
programs and services to Americans.

In the United States, marijuana is
a billion-dollar industry. Marijuana
is one of California's largest cash
crops, earning approximately $14
billion in sales annually. At present,
that money goes to drug dealers and

Canada's Billion-Dollar Business

The hemp plant has a long history throughout the world, and it remains an important crop. According to *Forbes* magazine, in 2003, Canada's cannabis crop was estimated in the billions, ranging from $4 billion to $7 billion. If that crop were managed by one company, it would exceed Apple Corporation in sales.

manufacturers who work outside the legal system and pay no tax on these earnings. Supporters of marijuana legalization estimate California alone could earn $1.3 billion per year in tax revenues on the legal sale of marijuana, if the tax were set at 10 percent. Taxes could be set even higher to generate more income. States often set flat tax rates for alcohol and tobacco. For example, a few states charge a tax of $2 per pack of cigarettes.

Taxation Equals Limitation

In addition to bringing in much-needed tax dollars for state and federal governments, taxing marijuana at high rates could discourage recreational users. Such high taxes could make marijuana too expensive to be used casually.

TAXATION AND REGULATION

Economist Jeffrey Miron of Harvard University advocates legalizing and regulating marijuana for financial gain. In 2005, Miron published "The Budgetary Implications of Marijuana Prohibition," a report in which he examined "the budgetary implications of legalizing marijuana—taxing and regulating it like other goods—in all fifty states and at the federal level."[1] The report includes estimates of savings to the government if marijuana were legal and taxed rather than illegal and not taxed. Miron wrote, "Replacing marijuana prohibition with a system of legal regulation would save approximately $7.7 billion in government expenditures on prohibition enforcement—$2.4 billion at the federal level and $5.3 billion at the state and local levels."[2] These figures are based on taxing marijuana at a level of most consumer goods. If the rate were higher, as for alcohol and tobacco, revenue from marijuana sales could be as high as $6.2 billion at the federal level.

Miron is not alone in endorsing taxation and regulation of marijuana. More than 500 economists support his report and its findings, including Nobel laureates. And proponents for marijuana taxation and regulation extend beyond economics experts.

Covered by Insurance

There have been cases in which people growing cannabis plants have been reimbursed by their insurers when their plants have been stolen or confiscated. Most of these cases have occurred in California, where medical marijuana is legal by state law.

Robert DeArkland is the first known recipient of reimbursement for lost cannabis plants via his homeowner's policy. Seventy-one-year-old DeArkland was using marijuana medicinally. In 1998, authorities took his plants, which ultimately died from lack of water. In September 1999, the resident of Fair Oaks, California, received $6,500 ($500 for each plant) from his insurer, CGU California Insurance, for his loss.

National Debt

In April 2009, Daniel Cwiakala wrote a letter to a newspaper in Ohio that had printed an article about legalizing marijuana to help the United States get out of its financial crisis:

"The article . . . makes the statement that if marijuana was legalized it could be used by the government as a 'source of tax revenue.' . . . Even if the government can get taxes off of it, these taxes will not help to fix the problem of our national debt. There is no way that even 6.2 billion dollars a year will help our nation out of debt. We will still be left with more than 11 trillion dollars of debt. . . . Even if the government would make money on tax revenue and save money on the 'war with marijuana,' who is to say they still would take this money and use it to reduce the national debt? There is no way that simply using money gained by the legalization of weed will save our economy."[4]

The Marijuana Policy Project (MPP) is a nonprofit organization fighting for the legalization of marijuana. With regard to the discussion of marijuana legalization and taxation, the MPP noted:

> *Just one year's savings would cover the full cost of anti-terrorism port security measures required by the Maritime Transportation Security Act of 2002. The Coast Guard has estimated these costs, covering 3,150 port facilities and 9,200 vessels, at $7.3 billion total.*[3]

Taxation and regulation supporters include average citizens as well. In July 2009, voters in Oakland, California, overwhelmingly approved (80 percent) a special tax on marijuana sales. Oakland has four dispensaries that legally distribute cannabis. Money from the recently approved 1.8 percent sales tax—possibly $300,000 in 2010—will go to Oakland's general fund.

While the possible financial gains of taxing marijuana are appealing, not everyone supports this view. For many opponents, the possible financial gains of taxation and regulation simply are not reason enough to make marijuana a legal substance. First, opponents point out that legalizing and taxing marijuana will not generate enough revenue to entirely eliminate state and national debts. Some believe that more money will need to be spent on rehabilitation and addiction treatment

History-Making Measure

On July 21, 2009, Oakland, California, made U.S. history. When voters there approved a marijuana sales tax, Oakland became the first U.S. city to have such a tax. Measure F asked voters, "Shall City of Oakland's business tax, which currently imposes a tax rate of $1.20 per $1,000 on 'cannabis business' gross receipts, be amended to establish a new tax rate of $18 per $1,000 of gross receipts?"[5] Eighty percent of the voters said yes.

For Dale Gieringer, California state coordinator for NORML, the election was a big step forward in the fight to legalize marijuana. Gieringer said, "The voters of Oakland have sent a message to the nation that cannabis is better treated as a legitimate, tax-paying business than as a cause of crime and futile law-enforcement expenditures."[6]

Opponents believe approval of Measure F is a step in the wrong direction. For them, the new law has increased the possibility of greater drug use and crime. Oakland will serve as a real-life case study of what can happen when marijuana is taxed. Depending on what happens with drug use, crime rates, and the city budget in Oakland in the near future, similar measures could be proposed nationwide. Using Oakland as the test case, time will reveal how such measures are worded and, if approved, how they will be implemented.

In 2009, voters in Oakland, California, approved a bill to tax medical marijuana sales at dispensaries. The tax will generate income for the city.

for marijuana users. Also, other economic sectors may see loss of productivity if marijuana use became common. Finally, some argue that black markets exist for legal substances, and even if marijuana were legal, some would find ways around paying mandated taxes.

A New Infrastructure

The numbers presented by those who support the economic advantages of legalizing marijuana are noteworthy. However, making marijuana a legal, taxed, and regulated substance would be only the first step in achieving the financial gains outlined in Miron's report.

If marijuana were legalized, an infrastructure surrounding the new industry would be necessary. The Bureau of Alcohol, Tobacco, and Firearms and the FDA are the two federal agencies largely responsible for regulating legal drug use in the United States. Decisions would have to be made regarding who would regulate marijuana. Perhaps an entirely new agency would be created. Some legalization opponents believe regulation would be unwieldy and

Environmental Benefits

The debate over hemp's usefulness has resurfaced. Its growth has the potential to boost more than the economy. Environmentalists see a value in growing hemp for industrial purposes. Hemp can be used to create paper, which could reduce the amount of trees cut down. In addition, growing hemp is believed to improve soil, so crops grown in fields after hemp is harvested can benefit from richer soil. Hemp is also naturally insect-resistant, which requires less use of harmful insecticides and pesticides that can damage water supplies.

ultimately unsuccessful. Extensive planning would be required to determine the framework of this new system, which could become as complicated and expensive as law enforcement is now. ⌐

Medical marijuana is legal in California. Danielle Schumacher teaches a class to prepare Californians for jobs in the marijuana industry.

More than 6,700 pounds (3,040 kg) of marijuana were found in a private home in Indiana. Many police resources go toward marijuana drug busts.

LAW ENFORCEMENT

*A*rguments about the economic benefits of legalizing marijuana include discussion of law enforcement. Supporters highlight how money spent on law enforcement could be saved and better spent elsewhere if marijuana were a legal substance. Opponents believe legalization constitutes approval of drug use and will increase use in current users and create new users. They believe many law-abiding citizens have resisted the temptation to try marijuana simply because it is illegal. They are concerned that if the law were to change, new users would emerge eager to try the drug.

REGULATION EQUALS GREATER SAFETY

Some supporters of marijuana agree that using marijuana can be harmful. But for them, this fact is all the more reason why marijuana should be made legal. As is, the illegal market operates away from any regulations, so there is no way to control the drug sellers and their product. These supporters of legalization argue that if marijuana were legal, as alcohol and tobacco are, the government could put laws in place to ensure that dealers do not distribute a dangerous product. For example, some marijuana sold illegally is laced with extremely harmful ingredients as fillers to bulk up the drug. Drug dealers may also mix other drugs into the marijuana to make it more potent—drugs that might be significantly more dangerous to both the user and others than marijuana itself.

If marijuana were legalized and regulated, national guidelines could eliminate the use of these dangerous impurities. Furthermore, people who buy marijuana illegally do not know in advance the strength of its THC concentration. Regulations could control and standardize THC levels, so buyers would be aware of the strength of the drug they were using.

"It is important to recognize that science is but one aspect of the medical marijuana controversy. Ultimately, drug laws must address moral, social, and political concerns as well as science and medicine."[1]

—Allison Mack and Janet Joy, Marijuana as Medicine? The Science Behind the Controversy

Marijuana Is a Gateway Drug

Some opponents of legalization believe marijuana is a gateway drug—it encourages users to try harder drugs, such as cocaine, heroin, methamphetamines, or ecstasy. They fear that the increased marijuana use caused by legalization will lead more people, especially young people, toward life-threatening drug abuse and addiction. This would put an increased strain on law enforcement officers to arrest and prosecute these users.

This claim is difficult to prove. Even if the majority of hard drug users began with marijuana, there is no evidence that marijuana caused them to pursue stronger, more addictive substances. Still, opponents of legalization say the safest policy is to simply take marijuana out of the equation.

The problem of gateway drugs is an issue of great concern to law enforcement officers, as well as parents, educators, and health-care workers. Many people agree that if marijuana leads to harder drugs, it should be discouraged. The possibility especially worries law enforcement officers, whose job it is to fight drug trade and abuse. Hard drug use and drug dealing has been proven to contribute to increased crime rates. In the eyes of some, blocking marijuana could help decrease crime, especially in urban areas.

Not surprisingly, people have various opinions regarding the concept of marijuana as a gateway drug. Some believe that it certainly is a gateway and should be outlawed for that reason alone. Others believe that it might be, but only because people who are willing to use marijuana possess an inclination toward harder drugs. There are those who believe it is not a threat to further drug use at all. Still others believe the biggest gateway drug is alcohol, which is already a legal substance.

Some marijuana supporters argue that it is not marijuana itself that serves as a gateway, but only the fact that it is illegal. Once users begin using one illegal substance, it is easy to justify trying another illegal substance. Therefore, legalizing marijuana would end this gateway. If marijuana became legal, a user would be less likely to think breaking the law is acceptable. Still, opponents argue that studying health effects of marijuana is not the only way to measure its harm. They say having a strong negative social effect is just as bad as the physical damage a drug may cause.

"A majority of prosecutors agree that the existing marijuana laws do not deter people from initiating use, or users from using regularly or from transferring small amounts for little or no consideration. The law enforcement officers' work involving marijuana is totally in vain, accomplishing nothing but placing people in a confrontational path with the law. At the same time, law enforcement's credibility in the community is jeopardized."[2]

—The Shafer Commission, in a report on marijuana policy released on March 22, 1972, under President Nixon

LOWER BURDEN ON LAW ENFORCEMENT

According to the Federal Bureau of Investigation statistics, one marijuana smoker is arrested every 45 seconds in the United States. Proponents of legalizing marijuana claim that valuable time and resources are wasted on enforcing laws against a drug that is not as dangerous as legal substances such as tobacco or alcohol.

Drug-sniffing canines are a resource used by the police to find illegal substances such as marijuana.

The United States spends approximately $150 billion each year on police and courts. In addition, more than $65 billion is spent on corrections and correctional institutions. Approximately one-third of people in jails and prisons have been convicted of nonviolent drug crimes.

Making cannabis illegal has undoubtedly created a justice system filled with marijuana users. Marijuana offenses account for nearly 48 percent of drug arrests. In 2007, state and local law enforcement officers throughout the country arrested 872,721 people for marijuana offenses. So many marijuana-related arrests occur each year that legalization would significantly alter the criminal justice system—financially and operationally. But whether the changes are for the better is unknown.

Supporters of marijuana legalization believe law enforcement has better ways to spend its time and resources than by arresting marijuana users. They cite the social acceptance and popularity of marijuana as evidence that the drug should be decriminalized. A high percentage of all drug-related arrests are due to marijuana possession and sale. These minor crimes waste countless hours of time and billions of dollars for both police and the courts, they say.

However, others point out that arresting marijuana users is an important step in preventing violent crimes. They maintain that arresting marijuana users deters irresponsible use of psychoactive, mind-altering drugs that could lead people to commit violent crimes.

NATIONAL SECURITY

Some supporters of marijuana legalization are more concerned about the large amount of unregulated marijuana that is smuggled into the United States. Much of the smuggled marijuana comes across the Mexican border. It was grown in Mexico or farther away in Central or South America. There is no way of knowing if the drug was grown and handled safely, cleanly, or responsibly.

When products cross the U.S. border legally, they are screened. For example, fruit and other produce are

Legalize or Decriminalize?

People use two terms when discussing marijuana and the law: *legalization* and *decriminalization*. Some people insist on legalization, in which case all marijuana use, sales, and manufacture would become legal. In this scenario, laws would likely regulate these aspects, as is the case for alcohol and tobacco.

Other people push for decriminalization. This would reduce the penalty for those who are found using, growing, or selling marijuana. In Massachusetts, for example, a person who is in possession of less than one ounce (28.3 g) of marijuana cannot be arrested. Instead of facing serious fines and jail time, people caught with marijuana would receive a citation, similar to a speeding ticket, and pay a small fine. Those in favor of such measures claim that past experience supports their case: people who live in places where marijuana is decriminalized use less or equal amounts of the drug than those in places where marijuana is illegal. This argument refutes accusations that decriminalization would increase marijuana usage.

Some people who advocate decriminalization view it as a step on the path to legalization, and others would be satisfied with decriminalization as an end in itself.

Replacing Alcohol with Marijuana

When the prohibition of alcohol ended in 1933, law enforcement agencies were restructured to accommodate the change in law. Today, legalization proponents look back at this time in history as a turning point in their cause. They suggest that the government was worried about the law enforcement personnel who would lose their jobs as a result of the change in legislation. In their view, marijuana was offered up as an alternative illegal substance. Drug agents employed during Prohibition could now fill their time pursuing and punishing marijuana users. Some people believe the need to keep police jobs created the negative view of marijuana that still exists today.

checked for problems such as insects, mold, and diseases. Such screening works to prevent U.S. consumers from becoming ill from contact with harmful products. It also helps prevent contamination through the introduction of nonnative bacteria and insects. Biological intruders can do serious damage to crops and to people who are not used to them.

Legalization, marijuana supporters say, would enable U.S. border control officers to screen the millions of pounds of imported marijuana that come into the country. Such screening would not only protect users, they say, but society as a whole would be protected from contaminants likely present in smuggled marijuana.

Changes in marijuana legislation could affect all levels of the marijuana "industry"—growers, users, law enforcement, and court officers—in many ways. But such changes will likely only occur if marijuana is made a legal substance.

In 2009, U.S. Customs and Border Protection in Texas seized food cans used to smuggle marijuana. The smuggler was a high school student.

Supporters of marijuana legalization have argued that because alcohol and tobacco are legal, marijuana should be as well.

LEGAL PERSPECTIVES

People disagree about the legitimacy and effectiveness of marijuana laws. Questions remain about whether these laws are just, add to public safety, and have benefits that outweigh the costs to law enforcement and the court systems.

Furthermore, disparities between federal laws and state laws can be confusing and complicated. Disputes continue about how severe laws should be, whether marijuana use is a criminal act, and how its use compares with other crimes, such as drug dealing, theft, and murder. These disputes are at the core of the debate regarding how people should be punished.

Alcohol, Tobacco, and Marijuana

Many supporters of marijuana legalization believe marijuana is safe for recreational use. They do not deny that it is a drug with mind-altering properties, but they believe that it is safer—or at least no more dangerous—than alcohol or tobacco, which are legal substances.

Marijuana advocates use statistics about alcohol- and tobacco-related accidents, illnesses, and deaths to make their point. They highlight that although hundreds of thousands of people die each year from complications related to alcohol and tobacco use

Safety in Numbers

Marijuana, alcohol, and tobacco are the three most popular drugs in the United States. NORML and other marijuana advocacy groups claim marijuana is nontoxic and cannot cause death by overdose. They quote the prestigious European medical journal, the *Lancet*: "The smoking of cannabis, even long-term, is not harmful to health. . . . It would be reasonable to judge cannabis as less of a threat . . . than alcohol or tobacco."[1]

or abuse, those substances are legal. They also state that it is impossible to overdose on marijuana. From their point of view, it is difficult to understand why marijuana is the illegal drug among the three.

If legalized, some people would like marijuana to be treated similarly to alcohol. Alcohol is legal for people over the age of 21, but laws punish irresponsible use. For example, a person can be arrested for driving under the influence of alcohol, for exhibiting drunk and disorderly conduct, or for selling or serving alcohol to underage users. Many would like to see similar laws for marijuana, while others believe marijuana is so safe that such regulation is unnecessary.

Still others would like to see marijuana penalties stay the same or become even harsher. Or they believe current marijuana laws should be more strictly enforced. Often, this opinion stems from the belief that for society to function, laws must be followed despite personal disagreement. Opponents also worry about the effect marijuana users and dealers will have on the community. They believe drug users should be kept away where they cannot have a negative influence on others—especially on children.

INDIVIDUAL RIGHTS

Some marijuana advocates believe that preventing its use is a violation of individual rights and free will. Even if the drug is dangerous, they say, the only danger is to the individuals who choose to use it. They believe the government does not have the right to stop people from engaging in personal behaviors.

Those who are for and against the legalization of marijuana may also have different understandings of the law and its purpose. There are differing beliefs about which is a higher priority:

Tracking the Relative Danger

Those who support the legalization of marijuana often state that the drug is no more dangerous than other substances that are legal, such as tobacco and alcohol. The Center for Disease Control and Prevention cites that each year in the United States, approximately 443,000 deaths can be attributed to cigarette smoking. Also, in each year from 2001 to 2005, approximately 79,000 people died from excessive alcohol use.

However, it is difficult to determine how many deaths are caused directly by marijuana each year. The MPP claims nobody has died from a marijuana overdose. Joycelyn Elders, former U.S. surgeon general under President Bill Clinton, wrote, "Unlike many of the drugs we prescribe every day, marijuana has never been proven to cause a fatal overdose."[2] Other statistics do point to traffic accidents in which drivers at fault were shown to have marijuana in their systems. In other cases, marijuana was suspected of contributing to death. Even still, a report by the Substance Abuse and Mental Health Services Administration noted, "Marijuana is rarely the only drug involved in a drug abuse death. Thus, . . . the proportion of marijuana-involved cases labeled as 'One drug' (i.e., marijuana only) will be zero or nearly zero."[3]

personal freedom or national safety. Some people
believe marijuana use falls under the purview of
privacy or freedom of expression, which are both
guaranteed by the Bill of Rights. They believe the
government is acting against the principles of the
U.S. Constitution by keeping marijuana illegal.
However, when individuals choose to drink alcohol
or smoke marijuana and drive, they put themselves
and those around them—passengers, pedestrians,
and other drivers—at risk. Using these substances
impairs the body, including judgment. As a result,
the choice of one can jeopardize the safety of many.

Mandatory Minimums

Each state has its own laws governing marijuana
use. Under federal law, a first offender possessing
any amount of marijuana faces a fine of $1,000
and up to one year in prison. For a second or third
offense, the person will face certain jail time of at
least 15 days, possibly up to three years. For larger
offenses, such as the sale or cultivation of marijuana,
violators face up to life in prison and multimillion
dollar fines.

A key issue in the legal debate over marijuana is
about mandatory minimum sentences.

Andrea Barthwell, a director in the Office of National Drug Control Policy, argues against Illinois legislation that would legalize medical marijuana.

A mandatory minimum is the least possible sentence for an offense. If the offense carries a mandatory minimum sentence, the judge cannot sentence the convicted person to less than the minimum. Mandatory minimums are in place so that judges cannot soften the punishment for a crime the federal government has deemed serious. Judges carry a variety of opinions about drug use, and mandatory minimums help regulate punishments for drug offenders.

Some mandatory minimum sentences for marijuana offenses include life in prison. Some supporters of legalization are pushing for a change in legislation. They argue that the rules do not grant judges the ability to allow for special cases or to tailor sentences to more appropriately fit the crimes. Another concern with mandatory minimums is that they require low-level drug offenders to do hard time alongside sometimes dangerous criminals. The MPP is working to change legislation because the organization "believes that the greatest harm associated with marijuana is prison."[4] Rather than incarcerate low-level offenders, the MPP is striving for legalization and regulation, which would result in marijuana policies that are nonpunitive.

Eliminating mandatory minimums would not only keep thousands of low-level offenders out of prison, it could help save millions of dollars. According to the nonprofit group Mandatory Madness, the percentage of drug offenders in federal prisons more than doubled as a result of mandatory minimums. From 1981 to 2001, the number of drug offenders in the prison population increased from

25 percent to 60 percent. At a cost of $22,000 per year to incarcerate a prisoner, this explosion in the prison population dramatically increased the expenses of the Federal Bureau of Prisons.

But removing mandatory minimums could result in increased drug use, opponents argue. Mandatory minimums ensure consistency, so similar crimes receive similar sentences. The sentencing guidelines deter drug sales and use because of the consistency of the consequences. Because the minimums result in prison time, people are less likely to use marijuana.

CONFLICTING LEGISLATION

But legislation varies nationwide. Because each state has its own laws regarding marijuana, medical use is acceptable in some states, such as California, but not others, such as Texas.

Minimums Do Not Equal Safer Streets

In March 2009, Maxine Waters, a representative from California, introduced a bill in the U.S. House of Representatives. H.R. 1466 would get rid of mandatory minimums for low-level drug offenders and give courts the power to determine how best to respond to these offenders. For example, a judge could parole an offender or even suspend his or her sentence. In addition, federal involvement in such cases could be limited. When introducing the bill, Waters explained, "Mandatory drug sentences have utterly failed to achieve Congress's goals. Longer sentences and more people in prison haven't translated into safer streets."[5] As of mid-2010, the bill was still under consideration.

Perhaps more confusing is the fact that, while marijuana use is legal in some circumstances in some states, federal law prohibits its use altogether. So, even though the state of California approves the use of medical marijuana, a user in San Diego could be arrested by federal agents for smoking cannabis.

Recent decisions by the U.S. Supreme Court have addressed this disparity. In 2005, the Court ruled in *Gonzales v. Raich* "that the federal government has the constitutional authority to prohibit marijuana for all purposes."[6] The Court did acknowledge the conflicting federal and state laws, and the justices recommended Congress work with the FDA to resolve the differences that exist between federal and state laws. The federal government has the authority to prosecute marijuana users based on federal laws, but it does not have to. The enforcement practices have changed based on the administration in place. Regardless of the law regarding marijuana use, not all citizens agree with it. The challenge to creating new marijuana legislation is that opinions and beliefs differ about what is right and wrong.

Alabama Attorney General Troy Kind believes that, ultimately, states should have the right to decide drug policies, not the federal government.

Angel Raich suffers from scoliosis, a brain tumor, and chronic pain. She says marijuana is the only medication that helps her.

RIGHT AND WRONG

For some participants in the marijuana debate, the issue of legalization comes down to a simple distinction: right and wrong. For these people, there is really no debate. The issue is black and white, not gray. Many of those who oppose marijuana use believe it is dangerous and the government should uphold this principle through its laws. Though there are arguments for the advantages of legalizing marijuana, including potential medicinal and economic benefits, opening the door to crime and drug-seeking behavior is not worth the added benefit for the few legitimate potential users.

Because some believe legalizing marijuana undermines society as a whole, they find it upsetting that lawmakers would even consider legalization. Some studies have shown marijuana use is related to reckless driving and lack of motivation, although it is unclear if marijuana is the only factor in those behaviors. Many people associate marijuana use with laziness, depression, and listlessness, attributes that are undesirable to communities and society.

Some opponents also believe legalization contradicts the values of U.S. society as a whole because they

Marijuana and the Church

Churches remain some of the staunchest anti-drug advocacy groups. In general, they consider recreational marijuana use wrong. In some religious circles, the moral ban on drugs extends to alcohol, tobacco, and even caffeine.

Some Christians are outspoken in their support of marijuana legalization, however. Christians for Cannabis is one such group. They seek to remove stereotypes associated with marijuana use and encourage citizens to seek medically accurate information when forming their opinions.

connect marijuana with crime and other negative behaviors. James A. Inciardi and Duane C. McBride addressed this issue, and others, in their article "Debating the Legalization of Drugs":

> *There are many disturbing questions about marijuana's effect on the vital systems of the body, on the brain and mind, on immunity and resistance, and on sex and reproduction. Recent research on behavioral aspects suggests that marijuana use severely affects the social perceptions of heavy users. . . .*

> *The study reported that the research subjects used marijuana to avoid dealing with their difficulties and that their avoidance inevitably made their problems worse—on the job, at home, and in family and sexual relationships.[1]*

"By characterizing the use of illegal drugs as quasi-legal, state-sanctioned, Saturday afternoon fun, legalizers destabilize the societal norm that drug use is dangerous. They undercut the goals of stopping the initiation of drug use to prevent addiction. . . . Children entering drug abuse treatment routinely report that they heard that 'pot is medicine' and, therefore, believed it to be good for them."[2]

—Andrea Barthwell, MD, Former Deputy Director, White House Office of National Drug Control Policy

Some people believe legalization would set a bad example for children. It will make it harder for parents to teach their children that drug use is dangerous. They challenge the ability of young people to learn what is bad for them if the government endorses a drug. These opponents are not soothed by the idea of government regulation over marijuana use. Rather, they think the message of legalization would override any attempts to control people's usage of the drug.

SOCIAL COSTS ARE GREATER THAN INDIVIDUAL RIGHTS

Legalization comes at a high social cost, opponents say. They disagree with the argument that using marijuana should be an individual choice. They believe laws exist to protect innocent members of society from the irresponsible decisions of others. In their view, marijuana use is a poor decision that affects more than those who engage in it.

For example, opponents note that the children of marijuana users may suffer. A parent who uses marijuana may be in an altered state of mind when he or she needs to be an active, attentive caregiver. Opponents believe increased usage of drugs resulting from legalization will lead to the neglect of children. Social services will have to step up to provide for these children, which will cause an added strain on public dollars.

Reporters Ethan Nadelmann and Jann S. Wenner wrote a response to such worries about children:

While driving under the influence of alcohol and marijuana, Michael Gagnon caused an accident that killed a mother and her four children.

Americans ask, "What about our children?" but they forget that virtually any kid—in any city, town or suburb—who wants to try drugs can find them easily right now. And still others say, "What about the message it would send?" but forget that our current response—insane antidrug efforts like "Just Say No" and "This is Your Brain on Drugs," along with our incredibly cruel laws—send far worse messages: that kids are stupid, that drug users are less than human, and that people who do no harm to others deserve to lose their freedom.[3]

MEDICAL ETHICS

The issue of right and wrong plays a major role in the practice of medicine. As part of their medical study, physicians are increasingly focused on ethics, or how moral values apply to medical issues. Areas that raise many questions in regard to medical ethics include stem cell research, doctor-assisted suicide, organ donation, and medical marijuana. These are high-stakes areas of medicine, where a physician's actions or lack of action may cause harm or even death to a patient.

An ancient rule many modern physicians follow is *primum non nocere*, which is Latin for "first, do no harm." A physician must consider the risk and possibility of inflicting harm to a patient before administering a procedure. Those who oppose medical marijuana wonder if prescribing it violates this rule.

The Hippocratic oath also deals with important issues of medical ethics. Graduating medical students today often pledge versions of the oath, which was likely written more than 2,000 years ago by Hippocrates, a Greek physician. One version contains a promise not to administer a deadly drug and to practice medicine with honor.

In the eyes of some, prescribing medical marijuana breaks these promises. After hearing about the Obama administration's policy to stop raiding medical marijuana dispensaries, Iowa Senator Chuck Grassley declared, "The first rule of medicine—'do no harm'— is being violated by the Attorney General with this decision."[4]

However, others believe it is immoral for a physician to withhold medicine from those who need it. If marijuana

California: A Case Study

The California State Board of Equalization estimates that taxing and regulating cannabis sales would raise approximately $1.4 billion in annual state revenue. This estimate is based on a $50-per-ounce tax on the retail sale of cannabis, as suggested in the proposed Marijuana Control, Regulation and Education Act. This act would tax the production, packaging, and sale of marijuana. Sales would be restricted to those over the age of 21. The bill would not alter existing legislation on the use of medicinal cannabis. New taxes would not apply to the medical cultivation of cannabis.

The study did not examine whether this act would reduce existing law enforcement and court costs, which California NORML estimates to be $200 million per year. In 2007, approximately 74,000 Californians were charged with marijuana offenses—a record number of arrests for one year since the state decriminalized possession in small amounts in 1976. In the report, the board speculated that some adult users may switch to marijuana from alcohol and cigarettes, thereby reducing the use of two other dangerous legal drugs.

One survey in California showed that 56 percent of respondents believe marijuana should be legalized for recreational use with proceeds taxed. Many wondered if this support increased because the state was facing a $26 billion budget deficit.

does have healing benefits, they say, it would be wrong to not help a patient use it. But even with a prescription, the patient would need legal means to acquire it. If a patient cannot acquire medicine, he or she may have to turn to illegal means to purchase it. Some people believe it is wrong to force ailing patients to have to turn to the black market to purchase legally prescribed marijuana.

LAWMAKERS RESPOND

In 2010, a number of state legislatures were considering legalizing medical marijuana, including Delaware, Illinois, Iowa, and New York. Each state was considering its own form of law. In New York, for example, legislation would allow physicians to prescribe marijuana only for specific ailments. It would also restrict patients' marijuana possession to certain amounts. In addition, other states were also discussing taking measures to legalize marijuana.

Legal Distribution in Rhode Island

In June 2009, Rhode Island became the second state to establish dispensaries for medical marijuana. It was only the second state after California to license and regulate distribution of medical marijuana. The bill allowing for this development was vetoed by the governor. Legislators overruled the veto with at least a two-thirds majority in the state house and senate.

No Easy Answers

Even without the change in federal policy under the Obama administration, the marijuana debate has been heated on both the state and federal levels. The broad public dialogue has gone hand-in-hand with ballot initiatives addressing marijuana legalization.

Society is facing the issue of legalizing marijuana not just in theory, but also in practice. The acceptance of medical marijuana by some communities has caused a shift in thinking for many people. Still, not everyone looks forward to changing legislation, and much is at stake. Laws would drastically alter the health care industries and law enforcement agencies. Both sides dispute the severity and impact of the consequences to society. What is known for sure is that this plant—this possibly dangerous, possibly useful cannabis plant—raises important questions with no easy answers.

Personal freedoms, economic impacts, right and wrong, and medical perspectives are all involved in the debate over legalizing marijuana.

TIMELINE

2800 BCE	1889 CE	1906
Records in China detail farming hemp for its fiber.	Botanist George Watt writes about the varieties of the cannabis plant.	Marijuana is classified as a dangerous drug under the Pure Food and Drug Act.

1937	1941–1945	1969
The Marihuana Tax Act begins to impose steep fines on all marijuana sales.	The Grow Hemp for Victory campaign engages midwestern farmers in growing hemp for the war effort.	President Richard Nixon makes the war on drugs a high priority.

1919

The Eighteenth Amendment to the U.S. Constitution prohibits alcohol.

1930

The Federal Bureau of Narcotics is created on August 12 to enforce drug laws.

1933

The Twenty-first Amendment to the Constitution ends Prohibition.

1970

Marijuana is labeled a dangerous drug under the Controlled Substances Act.

1971

The National Organization for the Reform of Marijuana Laws is founded as a lobbying group in Washington DC.

1973

The Drug Enforcement Administration is formed by combining the Federal Bureau of Narcotics and other drug prevention agencies.

TIMELINE

1985	1988	1992
The U.S. Food and Drug Administration approves Marinol, a synthetic drug containing THC.	DEA Judge Francis Young writes that medical marijuana is a safe therapeutic substance.	DEA officials override Judge Young's decision.

2007	2009
The onset of a worldwide economic crisis increases discussion of legalizing marijuana and taxing the sales for economic benefit.	In June, Rhode Island becomes the second state to establish dispensaries for medical marijuana.

1996	2005	2005
California legalizes marijuana for medical purposes.	Economist Jeffrey Miron publishes a report examining the potential tax benefits of legalizing and regulating marijuana.	The U.S. Supreme Court rules in *Gonzales v. Raich* that the federal government has the right to prohibit all marijuana use.

2009	2009
Oakland, California, becomes the first U.S. city to approve a marijuana sales tax by vote on July 21.	In October, the U.S. attorney general announces the federal government would not prosecute marijuana offenders who comply with state laws.

ESSENTIAL FACTS

AT ISSUE

Opposed

❖ Marijuana is dangerous, addictive, and harmful. People who use drugs affect more than just themselves; there is a high social cost to legalized drugs.

❖ People who abuse drugs may hurt others—on purpose or by accident.

❖ People should follow the law even if they do not agree with it.

❖ It is morally wrong to use drugs or to approve of their use.

❖ Medical prescriptions for marijuana are a cover for casual drug use.

❖ Marijuana is a gateway drug to harder substances.

In Favor

❖ Marijuana is a safe and natural substance that people have used for centuries. It is less addictive and harmful than alcohol or tobacco.

❖ Marijuana has medical benefits for people with serious illnesses.

❖ Taxing marijuana sales would bring new revenue to the economy.

❖ People should have the right to use drugs if they want to.

❖ Industrial hemp is useful and environmentally friendly.

❖ Legalizing marijuana would save time and money spent on law enforcement for small drug offenses.

CRITICAL DATES

1937

The U.S. Marihuana Tax Act began to impose steep taxes on marijuana use. This was the first attempt by the federal government to regulate marijuana. The taxes were so high that many physicians stopped prescribing marijuana to patients.

1985

Marinol, a synthetic drug that contains THC, was approved by the U.S. Food and Drug Administration. Opponents of legalization believe that with the availability of an FDA-approved THC pill, marijuana does not need to be legalized for medical use. Proponents of legalization believe THC is not a flawless substitute for medical marijuana.

2009

On October 19, U.S. Attorney General Eric H. Holder Jr. announced that under the Obama administration, the federal government would not prioritize prosecuting marijuana offenders. This was a change from the previous administration under George W. Bush, which had prioritized enforcing federal laws about marijuana.

Quotes

"The smoking of cannabis, even long-term, is not harmful to health. . . . It would be reasonable to judge cannabis as less of a threat . . . than alcohol or tobacco."—*Lancet*

"For those who are inclined to support medical use of marijuana, it is usually not the scientific evidence they consider, but only the unfounded self-reports of how marijuana relieved pain, chemotherapy-induced nausea and vomiting or HIV-AIDS Wasting Syndrome. . . . Proponents of the legalization of medical marijuana create the impression that it is a reasonable alternative to conventional drugs. But unlike conventional drugs, smokable marijuana has not passed the rigorous scrutiny of scientific investigation and has not been found safe and effective in treating pain, nausea and vomiting or wasting syndrome." —*Dr. Mark L. Kraus, Chapter of the American Society of Addiction Medicine*

ADDITIONAL RESOURCES

SELECT BIBLIOGRAPHY

Mack, Allison, and Janet Joy. *Marijuana as Medicine? The Science Behind the Controversy*. Washington, DC: National Academy Press, 2001.

Massing, Michael. *The Fix*. New York, NY: Simon & Schuster, 1998.

Matthews, Patrick. *Cannabis Culture: A Journey Through Disputed Territory*. London: Bloomsbury, 1999.

Rosenthal, Ed, and Steve Kubby. *Why Marijuana Should Be Legal*. New York, NY: Thunder's Mouth Press, 2003.

FURTHER READING

Loonin, Meryl. *Legalizing Drugs*. Farmington Hills, MI: Lucent, 2005.

Marcovitz, Hal. *Marijuana*. Farmington Hills, MI: Lucent, 2006.

Marijuana. Ed. Joseph Tardiff. Farmington Hills, MI: Greenhaven Press, 2008.

WEB LINKS

To learn more about legalizing marijuana, visit ABDO Publishing Company online at **www.abdopublishing.com**. Web sites about legalizing marijuana are featured on our Book Links page. These links are routinely monitored and updated to provide the most current information available.

For More Information

For more information on this subject, contact or visit the following organizations.

The Drug Enforcement Administration Museum
700 Army Navy Drive, Arlington, VA 22202
202–307–3463
www.deamuseum.org
The Drug Enforcement Administration Museum contains artifacts and exhibits relating to the history of drugs and current trends in drug use in the United States.

National Institute on Drug Abuse, Intramural Research Program
251 Bayview Boulevard, Baltimore, MD 21224
301–443–1124
www.drugabuse.gov
The National Institute on Drug Abuse conducts research to bring science and medical reason to the debate on drug use. It also works to make its research findings known on a broad scale.

The National Organization for the Reform of Marijuana Laws (NORML)
1600 K Street, Northwest, Suite 501, Washington, DC 20006
202–483–5500
www.norml.org
NORML is a nonprofit, public interest group that supports the responsible use of marijuana. The group lobbies politicians on behalf of marijuana supporters.

GLOSSARY

addiction
>An abnormal tolerance or dependence on a substance that produces withdrawal symptoms, such as headaches, if the substance is not taken.

cannabinoid
>A chemical found in marijuana that controls mental and physical processes.

cannabis
>The hemp plant; marijuana.

chronic
>Recurring.

controversy
>Debate or disagreement.

cultivate
>Grow.

decriminalize
>Lower the legal penalty.

dependency
>A physical or psychological reliance on a drug in order to function.

gateway drug
>A drug that leads its users to try more harmful drugs.

hemp
>The stalk portion of the *Cannabis sativa* plant.

mandatory minimum
>The least possible sentence for a drug crime that a judge must impose upon an offender.

Marinol
>Brand name for a laboratory-developed cannabinoid drug.

narcotics
>Strong mind-altering drugs.

over the counter
    Available for purchase by anyone.

pathogen
    Something, such as bacteria or a virus, that causes disease.

pot
    Popular slang term for marijuana or cannabis.

potency
    Strength.

precedence
    Priority or a high place of importance.

psychoactive
    Affecting the brain's function and perception.

resin
    Sap.

revenue
    Income.

synthetic
    Developed in a laboratory.

THC
    Tetrahydrocannabinol, the active ingredient in marijuana.

Source Notes

Chapter 1. Federal Policy Change
1. David Stout and Solomon Moore. "U.S. Won't Prosecute in States That Allow Medical Marijuana." *The New York Times*. 20 Oct. 2009. 11 Nov. 2009 <http://www.nytimes.com/2009/10/20/us/20cannabis.html>.
2. Ibid.
3. "Marijuana." *U.S. Drug Enforcement Administration*. 31 Aug. 2009 <http://www.justice.gov/dea/concern/marijuana.html>.
4. "About the Marijuana Policy Project." *Marijuana Policy Project*. 29 July 2009 <http://www.mpp.org/about/>.

Chapter 2. The Cannabis Plant
1. David P. West. "Hemp and Marijuana: Myths & Realities." *North American Industrial Hemp Council Online*. 24 Nov. 2009 <http://www.naihc.org/hemp_information/content/hemp.mj.html>.
2. Nick Brownlee. *The Complete Illustrated Guide to Cannabis*. London, UK: Sanctuary Publishing, 2003. 46.

Chapter 3. History of Cannabis Use and Laws
1. Peter T. Furst. ed. *Flesh of the Gods: The Ritual of Hallucinogens*. Prospect Heights, IL: Waveland, 1990. 235.
2. Ed Rosenthal and Steve Kubby. *Why Marijuana Should Be Legal*. New York, NY: Thunder's Mouth Press, 2003. 43.

Chapter 4. The Debate Begins
None.

Chapter 5. Medical Marijuana

1. Allison Mack and Janet Joy. *Marijuana as Medicine? The Science Behind the Controversy*. Washington, DC: National Academy Press, 2001. 4.
2. "What Is the Lethal Dose of Marijuana?" *Shaffer Library of Drug Policy*. 29 July 2009 <http://www.druglibrary.org/schaffer/library/mj_overdose.htm>.
3. "Report On Bills Favorably Reported By Committee." *Connecticut General Assembly*. 4 Apr. 2005. 16 Nov. 2009 <http://www.cga.ct.gov/2005/jfr/s/2005SB-00124-R00GL-JFR.htm>.
4. Paul Armentano. "Marinol vs. Natural Cannabis." *NORML.org*. 11 Aug. 2005. 24 Nov. 2009 <http://norml.org/index.cfm?Group_ID=6635>.

Chapter 6. Economics, Taxation, and Regulation

1. "Executive Summary." *Prohibitioncosts.org*. 24 Nov. 2009 <http://www.prohibitioncosts.org/execsummary.html>.
2. "Milton Friedman, 500+ Economists Call for Marijuana Regulation Debate; New Report Projects $10-14 Billion Annual Savings and Revenues." *Prohibitioncosts.org*. 24 Nov. 2009 <http://www.prohibitioncosts.org/execsummary.html>.
3. Ibid.
4. "How will legalizing weed improve America's economy?" *The Guardian Online*. 21 Apr. 2009. 24 Nov. 2009 <http://www.theguardianonline.com/opinion/how-will-legalizing-weed-improve-america-s-economy-1.1726582>.
5. Daniel B. Wood. "Oakland voters approve marijuana tax." *The Christian Science Monitor Online*. 22 July 2009. 24 Nov. 2009 <http://www.csmonitor.com/2009/0722/p02s07-ussc.html>.
6. Ibid.

Chapter 7. Law Enforcement

1. Allison Mack and Janet Joy. *Marijuana as Medicine? The Science Behind the Controversy*. Washington, DC: National Academy Press, 2001. 7.
2. Ed Rosenthal and Steve Kubby. *Why Marijuana Should Be Legal*. New York, NY: Thunder's Mouth Press, 2003. 20.

Source Notes Continued

Chapter 8. Legal Perspectives
1. "About Marijuana." *NORML.org*. 29 July 2009 <http://www.norml.org/index.cfm?Group_ID=7305>.
2. "Myths about Medical Marijuana." *Multidisciplinary Association for Psychedelic Studies*. 16 Nov. 2009 <http://www.maps.org/media/pj032804.html>.
3. "Mortality Data From the Drug Abuse Warning Network, 2001." *SAMHSA.gov*. 16 Nov. 2009 <https://dawninfo.samhsa.gov/old_dawn/pubs_94_02/mepubs/files/DAWN2001/DAWN2001_ME_A.pdf>.
4. "About the Marijuana Policy Project." *MPP.org*. 25 Nov. 2009 <http://www.mpp.org/about/>.
5. "Mandatory Madness." *Mandatorymadness.org*. 25 Nov. 2009 <http://www.mandatorymadness.org/>.
6. "Federal Marijuana Law." *Americans For Safe Access Online*. 25 Nov. 2009 <http://www.safeaccessnow.org/article.php?id=2638>.
7. Lee Davidson. "Chaffetz joins GOP's fight against drugs." *Deseret News*. 11 June 2009. 23 July 2009 <http://www.deseretnews.com/article/705315896/Chaffetz-joins-GOPs-fight-against-drugs.html>.

Chapter 9. Right and Wrong
1. James A. Inciardi, ed. *Handbook of Drug Control in the United States*. New York, NY: Greenwood Press, 1990. 290.
2. "Should Marijuana Be a Medical Option?" *ProCon.org*. 29 July 2009 <http://medicalmarijuana.procon.org/viewresource.asp?resourceID=000141>.
3. Ethan Nadelmann and Jann S. Wenner. "Toward a Sane National Drug Policy." *Rolling Stone*. 5 May 1994. 24–26.
4. Steve Benen. "Holder, Medical Marijuana, and GOP Ire." *Washington Monthly Online*. 19 Mar. 2009. 2 Dec. 2009 <http://www.washingtonmonthly.com/archives/individual/2009_03/017365.php>.

INDEX

INDEX CONTINUED

ABOUT THE AUTHOR

Kayla Morgan lives and writes in New York City. She studied history as an undergraduate and holds a Master of Fine Arts in writing. In addition to writing books for young readers, Morgan also speaks at schools and conferences around the country and teaches writing to teens and adults.

PHOTO CREDITS

Jan Priems/iStockphoto, cover, 3; David McNew/Getty Images, 6; Richard Hutchings/Photolibrary, 11; Scott J. Ferrell/Getty Images, 15, 99; Jorge Cubells Biela/Shutterstock Images, 16, 96 (top); Kathy Willens/AP Images, 19; Kelly Jordan/AP Images, 23, 97; David Dohnal/Shutterstock Images, 24; Getty Images, 29; AP Images, 33, 34, 43, 75; Alfred T. Palmer/Library of Congress, 39, 96 (bottom); Mel Evans/AP Images, 44; Marcio Jose Sanchez/AP Images, 49; Reed Saxon/AP Images, 55, 98 (top); iStockphoto, 56; Justin Sullivan/Getty Images, 62; Dino Vournas/AP Images, 65; Samuel Hoffman/AP Images, 66; Paul Bryant/AP Images, 71; Andrea Carolina Sanchez Gonzalez/iStockphoto, 76; Seth Perlman/AP Images, 81; Jamie Martin/AP Images, 85; Noah Berger/AP Images, 86, 98 (bottom); J.D. Pooley/AP Images, 90; Andre Blais/Shutterstock Images, 95